Getting

WHAT YOU WANT

BY FAITH

JOE-JESIMIEL OGBE

Getting What You Want By Faith

Copyright © 2016 by Joe-Jesimiel Ogbe

ISBN: 978-978-956-591-7

Published In Nigeria by

Young Disciples Press

3, YDI str, Off Isheri-LASU Rd, Hotel Bus Stop,

Igando-Lagos, Nigeria

01-2934286, 08023124455

www.ydiworld.org

joejesimiel2006@yahoo.com

All Scripture quotations are from the King James Version of the Bible, except otherwise stated.

Book Design & Printing In Nigeria:

Learnible

www.openlearnible.com

+234 8035215240

TABLE OF CONTENTS

DEDICATION

I sincerely dedicate this book to three of my most
outstanding Faith teachers:

Bishop David Oyedepo

Bishop David Abioye

Dr Frederick K. C. Price

Introduction

The US Dollar is one of the most popular currencies in the world today. Almost 85% of the total transactions in the foreign exchange market are done in this currency. USA has a very strong economy and can be called world strongest economy with the biggest bank in the world.

USA Dollar is the most used currency in the whole world, but not the most valuable. The most valuable currency in the world today is Kuwaiti Dinar, the official currency of Kuwait. It is considered as the highest value currency in the world and this is because Kuwait is a very rich country.

In the kingdom of God, the most valuable currency is faith. Our faith is a kind of currency that is accepted by God in exchange for whatever we want from Him. The world uses dollars and other currencies in exchange for goods and services. The more money you possess or have in this world, the greater your capacity to make purchases in the world. So also the more faith you possess, the greater your capacity to make "purchases" in the kingdom of God. Faith is what gets things done in the kingdom.

There is nothing you desire that faith cannot deliver into your hands! Faith has power to give you a child. Faith has power to give you spiritual, material and financial blessings. Faith has power to give you a career or business breakthrough. Faith has power to heal you and deliver you from every satanic attacks and oppressions. Faith has power to transform you from a nobody to somebody, from an ordinary person to an extraordinary person. Faith is it!

The truth of the matter is that whatever you want from God is already provided in the spiritual realm. But you can only take delivery of it on presentation of this valuable currency of faith. Everything in this world answers to money! The Bible says, "... but money answereth all things." (Ecclesiastes 10:19) You can virtually purchase anything that is manufactured or that you can commission to be manufactured, if you have enough money. In the economic system of the world, money is a determining factor, but not so in the economic system of heaven! Heaven does not recognize our money or earthly currency as a means of transaction. We don't come before God to get what we want with money in our hands or showing Him our evidence of money transfers which we have

2

made. No! But we can come before Him with faith in our hearts to get what we want.

The truth is that we all have been given a measure of this valuable currency of faith, but not many of us care to use it to get what we want from God. Many of us have failed to accept the truth that the more faith we have, the greater our capacity to get things from God. For example, many people who wanted healing desperately in the Bible only presented this valuable currency of faith to the Lord, and they all took delivery of their healing. Let's take a look at the following few examples:

The woman with an issue of blood

"And, behold, a woman, which was diseased with an issue of blood twelve years, came behind him, and touched the hem of his garment: For she said within herself, If I may but touch his garment, I shall be whole. But Jesus turned him about, and when he saw her, he said, Daughter, be of good comfort; thy faith hath made thee whole. And the woman was made whole from that hour." (Matthew 9:20-22)

A Canaanite Woman's Daughter

"But he answered and said, It is not meet to take the children's bread, and to cast it to dogs. And she said, Truth, Lord: yet the dogs eat of the crumbs which fall from their masters' table. Then Jesus answered and said unto her, O woman, great is thy faith: be it unto thee even as thou wilt. And her daughter was made whole from that very hour." (Mat 15:26-28)

The Centurion's Slave

"For I also am a man set under authority, having under me soldiers, and I say unto one, Go, and he goeth; and to another, Come, and he cometh; and to my servant, Do this, and he doeth it. When Jesus heard these things, he marvelled at him, and turned him about, and said unto the people that followed him, I say unto you, I have not found so great faith, no, not in Israel. And they that were sent, returning to the house, found the servant whole that had been sick." (Luke 7: 8-10)

A Lame Man at the Temple

"And his name through faith in his name hath made this man strong, whom ye see and know: yea, the faith which is by him hath given him this perfect soundness in the presence of you all." (Acts 3:16)

Faith is an instrument or force we engage to get what we want from God. For over three decades, God has graciously enabled me to trade this valuable currency of faith in exchange for heavenly blessings. God has moved me from faith to faith in the journey of life and ministry. With developed and imparted faith I was able to break the shackles of limitation. No matter the challenge, or difficulties I face in life and ministry, I choose consciously and concertedly to utilize or engage faith.

I can profoundly testify that it was my faith that delivered me from the plague of childlessness. I got married May 5th, 1990 to my lovely wife, and for nearly five years of marriage, we waited patiently for the fruit of the womb to no avail. My wife and I had to engage the force of faith practically to enforce our inheritance of fruitfulness as ably provided for all believers in the Holy Scriptures. I still remember vividly how I used to imagine and visualize my son eating with me on the dining table and how I used to speak to him even though he was not in sight.

One day I woke up with the consciousness that we needed to put action to our faith. Yes, we believed God was going to bless us with children. Yes, we have been confessing fruitfulness to no avail. To ensure the practicality of our faith, I urged my wife to always serve our son's food and place it near me on the dining table each time we had our meals, even when there was no son in sight to eat with. One day I invited one of my friends, Bamidele Edwards and his wife to have lunch with us after Sunday service in church. To me, this day was the climax of our faith practice in our quest to have our own biological children. My wife who was used to serving our son's meal in a small plate whispered to me from the kitchen whether she should still serve his meal as usual. To her, what we were doing was just a private faith practice. But I urged her to still go ahead and serve as usual. We were all served and I offered prayers and we started eating. Meanwhile, my friend and his wife were wondering in their heart who was going to eat the food in the small plate. They kept quiet but busy munching their food. Then after I finished my own food, I turned and said to the hearing of everyone on the dining table: "Son, should I help you finish your food?" And I started eating his food as though he was practically there with us.

After lunch my friend said to me, "My pastor, if God fails to give you a son then God is wicked. But I know that God is not wicked so I am confident our God will bless you with children, for I have not seen faith practiced this way before."

Truly, our God is not wicked! He is a loving Father who knows how to give good gifts to His children. The Bible says, "If ye then, being evil, know how to give good gifts unto your children, how much more shall your Father which is in heaven give good things to them that ask him?" (Mat. 7:11)

Today, through the currency of faith, God has graciously removed shame and reproach from our marriage by blessing us with three lovely sons. God is ever mindful of the various challenges we go through in life. Are you trusting God for the fruit of the womb? Maybe, people have called you barren or childless. I want you to refuse or reject the appellation given to you by man! Barrenness is not your name or portion! God who did it for my wife and I, will do it for you. You can get what you want from God by faith!

This book is my humble attempt to provoke you and others to become desperate for a change of status or situation by deliberately choosing the path of faith. You see, in this journey of life, lots of people know what they want out of life, but very few people actually engage the force of faith to get what they want. Knowledge alone is not enough. You must take action and it takes faith to take action.

I may not be telling you something new or fantastic about faith, but what if, you are reminded of what you already know, and then you're motivated to operate in faith! I am not sharing with you to show how successful I have walked in faith and succeeded. NO! I am not yet there. I have not yet arrived at my destination. But I can tell you candidly that each time I have met a quagmire or I wanted something desperately, I had to engage my faith in the right direction. As you read this book, may the spirit of faith which I carry cause you to overcome all your life challenges and also trigger you to get things beyond your wildest imagination.

A wise man said, "It's not what we do once in a while that shapes our lives but what we do consistently." We need to use the currency of faith consistently, not once in a blue moon. The Bible says "the just shall live by his faith." Faith is a valuable currency for everyday living! Imagine living in a country without money to exchange for goods and services! You will surely live like a destitute or a vagabond.

Nothing happens in our world without faith. No one will ever fulfill his or her divine destiny outside of faith. Lack of faith has made Christians to miss out on their destiny or true callings in life. If you don't want to remain a nonentity or ineffective in the race of life, you must decide now to work on your faith.

Truly, this book is different! It is loaded with timeless truths and insights on the subject of faith. As such, you must approach it with correct mindset. I like to advise that you read it prayerfully, because I have asked God to use the book to impart you with the spirit of faith, such that you will be empowered to get what you want from God.

Joe jesimiel Ogbe

October, 2016

Lagos

01

Chapter One

WHAT IS FAITH?

"Now faith is the substance of things hoped for, the evidence of things not seen." (Heb 11:1)

Faith has a plethora of definitions! In this chapter I would crave your indulgence to elucidate some of them for our consideration. According to Wikipedia, "faith is confidence or trust in a person or thing that is not seen; or the observance of an obligation from loyalty; or fidelity to a person, promise, engagement; or a belief not based on proof."

In the New Testament, the English word faith is used to translate the Greek word pistis. The New Strong's Expanded Dictionary of Bible Word says, "Pistis is used of belief with the predominate idea of trust (or confidence) whether in God or in Christ, springing from faith in the same.

The Bible also defines pistis in Hebrews 11:1, "Now faith is the substance of things hoped for, the evidence of things not seen." Faith is the substance or assurance of things we hope for, but have not yet received. Faith (confidence, belief, trust) is also our evidence of that which is not seen—the invisible spiritual things. Faith comes before a prayer is answered or before an individual has received what he or she has requested from God. If we have received what we asked for, then faith is not needed.

In Matthew 9:27-30, two blind men came to Jesus and asked Him to heal them. Jesus first asked them, "Do you believe that I am able to do this?" and their reply was, "Yes, Lord." "Then He touched their eyes saying, 'According to your faith let it be to you.' And their eyes were opened." Their faith and assurance that Jesus could give them sight was the substance or reality they hoped for. It also gave them the evidence or trust that they would receive what they asked for. They believed; that is, they had faith in advance that it would be done.

Faith is our ability to have a firm trust or confidence in something or someone we cannot really explicitly prove. For instance, none of us can empirically prove God but we have a firm trust that He exists and that He is a rewarder of those that diligently seek Him. The Bible says, "But without faith it is impossible to please him: for he that cometh to God must believe that he is, and that he is a rewarder of them that diligently seek him" (Heb 11:6).

Faith is actually relying on the fact that something is true. A chair is often used to help illustrate this. Many of us intellectually agree or recognize the existence of a chair, and even agree that it is designed to support a person who sits on it. Faith is taking action to sit on it.

Many of us usually think of faith in terms of religious beliefs, (strong belief in God or deity) and that is what faith is. But in the most basic sense, faith is complete trust or confidence in someone or something. For instance, flying will require a measure of faith, that is, complete trust in the pilot and the aircraft. Every airline passenger must operate faith in order to fly! He or she must have faith in the pilot's abilities to fly the aircraft. The passenger must have faith that the plane has been adequately maintained. He or she must also have faith that the weather conditions are safe enough to fly that day. I have travelled to some countries of the world, and I can tell you that I have never bothered myself to check the pilot's training, nor cared about the maintenance records of the aircraft. I just believed that everything will be fine. The truth is that millions of people who travel by air every year, do have a measure of faith in pilots and the planes they fly, if not they will never board.

Whatever or whoever you believe in will shape your life. That's why the subject of faith is critical and germane to you. Faith is your ticket or access to getting things you want. If you believe that God as your Heavenly Father will give you what you want, you are correct. If you also believe you are not qualified to get anything from Him, you are also correct. It shall be unto you according to your faith!

It is faith that gives you the surety to know that you will achieve your goals and objectives. Faith is your surest energizer or motivator. According to Anthony Robbins, in his powerful book, Unlimited Power, "The real horror of ghetto life is not the daily frustrations and deprivations. People can overcome those. The real nightmare is the effect the environment has on beliefs and dreams. If all you see is failure, if all you see is despair, it's very hard for

you to form the internal representations that will
foster success."

Through faith, God has helped me to succeed where
others thought was a no-go area due to the operations
of the forces of darkness. For instance, a minister of
God was virtually chased out of town via satanic
attacks and operations. But riding on the wings of
testimony of how God's servant, Bishop Oyedepo
dominated and dealt with witches and wizards in Ota,
I too decided that I would not give in to any gang up
from hell. Today God has honored my faith, as He is
fighting and winning all my battles.

With faith I was able to tap the richest resources in
God. There is no limitation with God! There is no
limitation with faith! I don't allow fear or unbelief to
limit me. What is fear? Fear is confidence that
something bad would occur or happen. What is faith?
Faith is confidence that something good would
happen. I always believe something good with
happen to me and my ministry! I believe God's
thoughts concerning me are good thoughts.

If only you and I can dare believe God, no matter the
deterioration of issues bothering us, or no matter the
precarious circumstances we are in, we will see the

glory of God. Beloved, every precarious situation or circumstance has expiry date. Lazarus was dead for four days and Jesus stepped in and made a difference. The Bible says, "Jesus therefore again groaning in himself cometh to the grave. It was a cave, and a stone lay upon it. Jesus said, Take ye away the stone. Martha, the sister of him that was dead, saith unto him, Lord, by this time he stinketh: for he hath been dead four days. Jesus saith unto her, Said I not unto thee, that, if thou wouldest believe, thou shouldest see the glory of God?"

(John 11:38-40)

Do you need an all-purpose key to open all closed doors? Faith is it! If faith could bring Lazarus back life, then faith is a very powerful force on the earth. A life devoid of faith is a life that is replete with struggles. Faith is all it takes for you to take delivery of your portion in life. With faith as your key tool, you will flourish like a palm tree, while others are famished. It is your faith that guarantees your distinction.

Many people believe certain facts about Jesus Christ. But knowing those facts to be true is not what the Bible means by "faith." Believing that Jesus is God incarnate who died on the cross to pay the penalty for our sins and was resurrected is not enough. Even the demons "believe" in God and acknowledge those facts. "Thou believest that there is one God; thou doest well: the devils also believe, and tremble."

(James 2:19)

We must personally and fully rely on the death of Christ as the atoning sacrifice for our sins. We must "sit in the chair" of the salvation that Jesus Christ has provided. This is saving faith. The faith God requires of us for salvation is belief in what the Bible says about who Jesus is and what He accomplished and fully trusting in Jesus for that salvation.

According to Bishop David Oyedepo, Africa's Apostle of faith, "Faith is our unshakable confidence in God and His word. Faith is engaging the word of God in order to enforce the delivery of your destiny"

In total concord with this definition, I was able to locate God's word in Luke 10:17, "And the seventy returned again with joy, saying, Lord, even the devils are subject unto us through thy name." and from that time till today, my faith for journey mercies has been concretized that I never entertain any iota of fear of accident when I go on missions. Instead, I have this resolute and absolute faith that I would return to base like "the seventy returned" with testimonies.

It is the word of God that we anchor our faith on to get what we want or to enforce the delivery of our desires. Faith is not just believing that God can give us what we want or ask of Him, it is being moved to do something to prove that we believe His word that we located. For instance, when I was moved or provoked to tell my wife to serve my son's food, and I ate the food on his behalf, my action demonstrated my faith, which moved God to give us a son. My action was a validation of my active or living faith. Is your faith living or dead? Your faith is dead if you merely talk without action! Your faith is dead if you only quote or read the Bible without applying it in your life.

Action is the hallmark of faith. We can claim or quote all the scriptures on prosperity, without getting anything near prosperity if we fail to do what engenders prosperity. We can claim or quote all healing scriptures, without healing if we fail to do what engenders healing. Bishop David Oyedepo eminently stated that, "Faith is not making God responsible for the happenings, faith is showing responsibility with God in the light of scriptures to create your desired future." In the school of faith, we have a role to play, it is only after we have played our role or part that we commit God to play His own role or part. Faith has joint responsibility! That's why Bishop Oyedepo thundered, "Any faith that seeks to make God absolutely responsible for the events of your life is an irresponsible faith."

Faith is also about our persuasion! Abraham was fully persuaded about the faithfulness of God to fulfill His promise! Abraham against all hope believed God's promise. He was not weak in faith at all, neither did he waver through unbelief regarding the promise of God but was strong in faith. He was fully persuaded that God had power or capacity to do what He had promised. "And being not weak in faith, he considered not his own body now dead, when he was about an hundred years old, neither yet the deadness of Sara's womb: He staggered not at the promise of God through unbelief; but was strong in faith, giving glory to God; And being fully persuaded that, what he had promised, he was able also to perform." (Romans 4:19 - 21)

Abrahamic type of faith springs from a transforming trust in the eternal promises of a God who cannot lie. Faith is a conscious choice to reach out and trust the promises of God. It is our complete trust, strong belief in God to do what we want Him to do for us.

We can't trust God and not take an action or step that authenticates our faith. Check out "action-words" as engaged by the following faith heroes:

- By faith Abel OFFERED a precious gift to God.
- By faith Enoch WALKED with God.
- By faith Noah BUILT an ark in obedience to God.
- By faith Abraham LEFT his father's house.
- By faith Isaac PLANTED during famine.
- By faith Moses REFUSED the comfort of Pharaoh's palace.

Faith is total reliance on another person to do that which you could never do for yourself. When someone is sick and taken to the hospital for treatment, he must totally rely heavily on the medical personnel if he really wants attention and remedy. He must have faith in his doctors to command results. So also we cannot save ourselves from our sins and iniquities. We cannot become children of God by our power, hence our need for Jesus Christ.

Christianity is a faith-based religion. It is based on faith in God and in His Son, Jesus Christ. God has provided us with His Word, the Holy Bible, as a testimony of His faithfulness to His people all throughout history. Christianity is faith in the person and work of Jesus Christ. When we place our faith and trust in Christ alone for our salvation, God takes our sin and places it on the cross of Christ and awards us, by grace, with the perfect righteousness of Christ. That, in a nutshell, is the Christian message.

Having received Jesus Christ as my personal Lord and Savior, I have an assurance of salvation today because of my transforming trust in the ability, power and capacity of God to save me through His Son Jesus Christ. I can depend on His promises, He's got the power or ability to deliver on His promises. When God makes a promise, it is utter foolishness and absolute unbelief on my part to wonder how He will keep His word. Faith does not reckon with "how." Faith believes and leaves the "how" in the hands of Almighty God.

Faith is a choice! It is a conscious choice to reach out and trust the promises of God that come to us through the death and resurrection of Jesus. The Bible says, "Blessed be the God and Father of our Lord Jesus Christ, which according to his abundant mercy hath begotten us again unto a lively hope by the resurrection of Jesus Christ from the dead," (1 Peter 1:3)

Do you really want to receive Jesus Christ as your Lord and Saviour like I did several years ago? If yes, then pray this simple prayer of salvation:

"Father God, I know that I have broken your laws and my sins have separated me from You. Please have mercy on me and forgive me all my sins. I believe that your Son, Jesus Christ died for my sins, He was resurrected from the dead and He is alive. I invite Jesus to become the Lord of my life, to rule and reign in my heart from this day forward. I hereby place my trust on the Lord Jesus to save me eternally. I ask that You send Your Holy Spirit to help me obey You, and to do Your will for the rest of my life. In Jesus' name I pray, Amen."

If you have prayed this prayer of salvation with true conviction, then you have been empowered to become a child of God and a true follower of Jesus.

This salvation work is the doing of God, and not of man! The Bible says, "But as many as received him, to them gave he power to become the sons of God, even to them that believe on his name: Which were born, not of blood, nor of the will of the flesh, nor of the will of man, but of God." (John 1:12-13)

Welcome to the family of God!

May I encourage you right now to find a Bible based church where you can attend regularly and concertedly with a view to growing in the knowledge of God through His Word, the Bible.

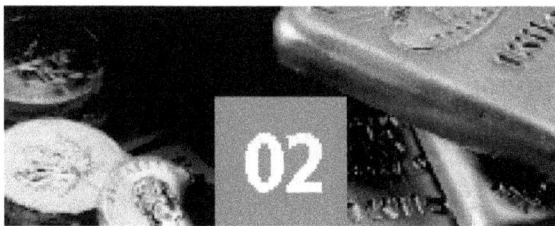

Chapter Two

WORTH OF FAITH

"But without faith it is impossible to please him: for he that cometh to God must believe that he is, and that he is a rewarder of them that diligently seek him." (Heb 11:6)

Worth of faith is about the value or importance of faith. There are reasons why I believe faith is important. For instance, in the light of the above scripture, faith is important because we cannot please God outside of faith. If we must please God we must engage or activate our faith.

Let's consider seven reasons why faith is very important:

1. Impossible becomes Possible

Faith is important because with your faith you can make an impossible case become possible! No impossibility can survive where faith is at work! The Bible says, "And Jesus said unto them, Because of your unbelief: for verily I say unto you, If ye have faith as a grain of mustard seed, ye shall say unto this mountain, Remove hence to yonder place; and it shall remove; and nothing shall be impossible unto you." (Mat.17:20)

Faith is important because it is your faith that enables you to operate in the class of God! As nothing is impossible with God, so also with faith. There is no impossibility with faith!

"For with God nothing shall be impossible."

(Luke 1:37) "Jesus said unto him, If thou canst believe, all things are possible to him that believeth." (Mark 9:23)

26

2. Salvation by Faith

Faith is important because without your faith you would not have been saved or born again. It is faith that procures salvation to humanity. The Bible says, "For by grace are ye saved through faith; and that not of yourselves: it is the gift of God: Not of works, lest any man should boast." (Eph. 2:8-9)

3. Justification by Faith

Faith is important because without it, you and I will not be justified before God. No one is justified before God on account of keeping the laws of God. We are all justified by our faith in the finished work of Christ on the cross of Calvary. "But that no man is justified by the law in the sight of God, it is evident: for, The just shall live by faith." (Gal.3:11)

4. Living by faith

Living by faith is living by the Word.

God told Joshua to march around the city 7 times by faith, not by his logic or reasoning. He had to live by the Word from God, not his perception of how illogical the command might have been for him and his army. Living by faith is living as though the goal has already been achieved. "Now the just shall live by faith: but if any man draw back, my soul shall have no pleasure in him. But we are not of them who draw back unto perdition; but of them that believe to the saving of the soul." (Heb. 10:38-39)

5. Kept by Faith

Faith is important because we are kept by faith! The Bible says, "Blessed be the God and Father of our Lord Jesus Christ, which according to his abundant mercy hath begotten us again unto a lively hope by the resurrection of Jesus Christ from the dead, To an inheritance incorruptible, and undefiled, and that fadeth not away, reserved in heaven for you, Who are kept by the power of God through faith unto salvation ready to be revealed in the last time" (1 Peter 1:3-5)

6. Healing by Faith

Faith is important because our healing is secured or procured by faith! For instance, it was the faith of the two blind men that secured their healing. "And when Jesus departed thence, two blind men followed him, crying, and saying, Thou Son of David, have mercy on us. And when he was come into the house, the blind men came to him: and Jesus saith unto them, Believe ye that I am able to do this? They said unto him, Yea, Lord. Then touched he their eyes, saying, According to your faith be it unto you. And their eyes were opened; and Jesus straitly charged them, saying, See that no man know it."

(Mat. 9:27-30)

7. Victory by Faith

Our victory in the world is secured on the platform of our faith in God. "For whatsoever is born of God overcometh the world: and this is the victory that overcometh the world, even our faith." (1 John 5:4) The devil knows the value or worth of faith, that's why he is busy blinding the minds of people out there. "In whom the god of this world hath blinded the minds of them which believe not, lest the light of the glorious gospel of Christ, who is the image of God, should shine unto them." (2Cor 4:4)

Faith is important because without faith it is impossible to overcome or gain victory over the devil and his cohorts. Nobody can quench all the fiery darts of the wicked by human power or means. But we can only cage the enemy by our resolute faith in the ability of God to battle on our behalf. "Above all, taking the shield of faith, wherewith ye shall be able to quench all the fiery darts of the wicked." (Eph. 6:16)

May your faith, which is your expression of resolute confidence in God and His Word not be thwarted. May you always be motivated by the Word of God in your daily walk with Him. May your faith as a spiritual force transport you from the natural realm to the supernatural and from humanity to divinity in Jesus name!

Chapter Three

GROWING IN FAITH

"We are bound to thank God always for you, brethren, as it is meet, because that your faith groweth exceedingly, and the charity of every one of you all toward each other aboundeth;"

(2 Thessalonians 1:3)

Like I stated in the preceding chapter, if you really want something great from God, or you want to matter to your world, then you better accept my counsel to work on your faith with a view to developing it. Don't be careless about the state or health of your faith. It is a tragedy to have a moribund faith, I mean a faith lacking vitality, vigour and growth. How can you still be celebrating the past achievements and victories of your faith, when you are supposed to have moved on to greater exploits via developed faith. If you don't want to experience defeat in life, then you must become desperate for faith development. You must develop or grow your faith; make sure your faith is growing exceedingly; and that you are increasing from faith to faith, not from faith to fear.

Undeveloped faith will stagnate or retrogress you, while developed faith has the capacity to move you forward pragmatically and progressively. You will achieve or obtain what you want in life only in proportion to the growth or development of your faith. Developed faith will bring increase of God's power and blessings into your life.

I said in my book, "The youth God uses" that to remain a toddler in Christ is to remain useless or of no value to God and His kingdom! If you desire to be useful to God, you must make up your mind to grow unto maturity. You cannot remain a baby in the Lord and expect to command signs and wonders. And you require developed faith to do signs and wonders. Your faith must grow because the issues you faced yesterday may not be the same today. The faith of yesterday is gone with yesterday. You need fresh faith to tackle fresh challenges and demands of life. In our ministry there were times in the beginning that we were using a measure faith to procure thousands of naira, but today we cannot dare to use that same measure of faith. We must graduate from a measure of faith to little faith in order to command millions! For us to move on to the level of greater exploits, we must consciously ask God for greater level of faith.

Understanding levels of faith

Faith has levels! There is a level of faith you get into that you get things from God cheaply. Let's consider three levels of faith:

1. No faith level

"And he said unto them, Why are ye so fearful? how is it that ye have no faith?" (Mark 4:40)

This "No faith" level is replete with fear! If you don't have faith then you have fear! Your faith is nonexistent, in comatose or dead! You need a living faith to enforce the delivery of your covenant blessings.

2. Little Faith level

"And Peter answered him and said, Lord, if it be thou, bid me come unto thee on the water. And he said, Come. And when Peter was come down out of the ship, he walked on the water, to go to Jesus. But when he saw the wind boisterous, he was afraid; and beginning to sink, he cried, saying, Lord, save me. And immediately Jesus stretched forth his hand, and caught him, and said unto him, O thou of little faith, wherefore didst thou doubt?" (Mat.14:28-31)

Little faith level is replete with doubts. Christians operating with little faith cannot confront great challenges, neither can they procure great things from God. That is why we must embrace the responsibility to develop our faith regularly and consistently.

3. Great Faith Level

"Then Jesus answered and said unto her, O woman, great is thy faith: be it unto thee even as thou wilt. And her daughter was made whole from that very hour." (Mat. 15:28)

Great faith level is replete with confidence, trust in the capacity of God to intervene in your affairs. This is the level God wants for all His children. Great faith will always have it the way it wants. Great faith will always put you in charge of the situation. I call this great faith as the "Commander's faith." It is the faith that commands results effortlessly! No faith level will command no results, while a measure of faith will give you a measure of results. Little faith level will give you little results, while great faith level will command great results! Which level do you prefer? The choice is yours!

To grow from "No faith" level to "Great faith" level you must embrace:

Word Intake

If you want great things from God, then accept personal responsibility to start right now to work on your faith by feeding on the word of God voraciously. Because the word of God is the authentic source of faith. Your faith will grow on the platform of word intake. The more of His word you take into your spirit the more your faith grows. Faith feeds on the word! More word more faith! You must devote your time and energy to reading, hearing and studying the word of God regularly, deliberately and concertedly.

Your faith grows as you meditate on God's word. Meditation is your resolve to think deeply and seriously about what you have read or memorised.

Learn to ask the Holy Spirit to guide and direct you into parts of scriptures that will help grow your faith.

A couple of years ago l found myself at a crossroad, not knowing what to do, the Holy Spirit led me to this particular Bible passage: "For I was ashamed to require of the king a band of soldiers and horsemen to help us against the enemy in the way: because we had spoken unto the king, saying, The hand of our God is upon all them for good that seek him; but his power and his wrath is against all them that forsake him. So we fasted and besought our God for this: and he was intreated of us." (Ezra 8:22-23) The testimony is that it was the exact word I needed at such an auspicious time.

Voice of God

Have you ever heard the voice of God?

Your capacity or ability to hear His voice will engender your faith growth. Your faith grows or develops when God speaks to you by an audible voice, or by a still small voice. I have been privileged to hear God's voice audibly. Sometime in 1983, I heard His audible voice, which I obeyed and I got delivered from death. He has also spoken to me via the still small voice! For instance, when our ministry was getting close to five years I started believing God for a plot of land but we couldn't afford it. But during the preparation for our 6th anniversary, God spoke these promising words: "You are six, what stops Me from giving you 6 plots of land in Lagos as your 6th anniversary gift." My faith instantly received a boost and I promptly announced to our missionary team what I heard from the Lord. None of them doubted or asked why six plots when we could not afford one plot. With faith in my heart, I simply took a step of faith and God honored my faith. Try your best by developing your spiritual ears to hear the voice of God when He speaks to you. God treasures speaking to His children.

Obedience

Obedience is key to faith growth. From personal experience, I can candidly say that obeying God's word is easy when you truly heard Him. When God spoke to me about six plots, even though we did not have enough fund to buy even one plot of land, I still obeyed by acting on what I heard that same hour. I did not wait till the following day! No! It was that same hour that I mobilized my staff to go in search of six plots. Today our youth ministry headquarters is situated on an acre - plus land in Lagos. To God be all the glory!

Some years back, my wife was believing God for a change of car. She listened to a tape on faith for instant miracle by Bishop David Oyedepo which boosted her faith. Same period, she was blessed with some pounds which she needed so badly to solve some issues, but was led by the Holy Spirit to sow the money as a seed faith. After initial inhibitions, she obeyed. The following day, she was blessed with enough money to change her car from quarters she least expected. Obedience is germane to faith development and performance, while disobedience will hamper your faith from performing optimally. Faith cannot be released in an atmosphere of disobedience.

The moment you disobey God's word to you, your progress in faith development stops at that level. Faith cannot grow or increase beyond your obedience. This is an immutable law of faith!

As your faith develops, your ability to trust and obey God grows. If you can't trust God for one million naira, how can you trust Him for ten million! You have not prayed and healed someone with headache with your faith; how do you think you can pray and heal someone with cancer.

Action

Faith cannot develop until it has been acted upon.
Each time you hear and act as I did, you take another
step in faith development. Until you put God's word
into action, your faith will not grow! It is your action
that defines your faith. It is your action that releases
the virtue that gets your faith to produce substance.
The power of faith is at the mercy of your Word-
provoked action. Faith is doing the Word of God.
"His mother saith unto the servants, Whatsoever he
saith unto you, do it." (John 2:5)

It is not only our words that matter to heaven, our
actions equally matter. He weighs our actions to see if
we truly operate in faith. "Talk no more so exceeding
proudly; let not arrogancy come out of your mouth:
for the LORD is a God of knowledge, and by him
actions are weighed." (1 Sam. 2:3)

Action is the only way to prove that you believe. If
you do not act out what you claim to believe, then
you don't believe it.

Fellowship

Fellowship remains a very vital spiritual force or
energy that helps our faith to grow. There is power in

fellowshipping with other Christians. Holy Spirit carries out His ministry in an atmosphere of fellowship. "And when they had prayed, the place was shaken where they were assembled together; and they were all filled with the Holy Ghost, and they spake the word of God with boldness." (Acts 4:31)

It is through fellowship that we connect with the Spirit of Christ, even as we provoke one another to growth via encouragement, edification and exhortation.

Fellowship is God's idea or mechanism for our spiritual health and wellbeing. And our spiritual health is defined by the health of our faith. A person with sick faith cannot connect spiritually with God.

Fellowship helps us to spur one another to live a life of faith. If you are in the dangerous habit of absenting yourself from fellowship your faith will not experience growth.

Testimony from others

In churches or fellowships, we gather together to worship God and to hear His word from anointed vessels. We also share testimonies of how God has graciously blessed us. The truth of the matter is that testimonies have the power to inspire and build our faith. For instance, when you hear of what God has done for your brother or sister in the Lord, you are motivated to stretch out your faith to connect with your own blessings too. Testimonies give you something to aspire to. Each time you hear testimonies from others you become expectant and hopeful that you too could be a beneficiary since God is not a respecter of persons. It is through testimonies that we learn the steps others have taken and we are provoked to take same steps with a view to procuring same testimonies.

We can't have issues dealing with current issues if we remember what has happened in the past. For instance, David had no issues confronting Goliath because he looked at what God did for him in the past. Faith is not a feeling. It's a decision. It's a choice! David chose to believe the Lord God of Israel and God gave him the head of Goliath. We all need to build faith in order to confront the Giants or Goliaths of life.

Apostolic Strategy

"And the apostles said unto the Lord, Increase our faith." (Luke 17:5)

What is the apostolic strategy here? It is the strategy of earnestly and honestly asking the Lord to intervene in your faith growth desires and endeavors. The apostles knew they were in short supply of faith. They knew they did not have enough of faith. What did they do? They decided to pray or call on the Lord to intervene. We too can grow our faith by asking God to increase our faith!

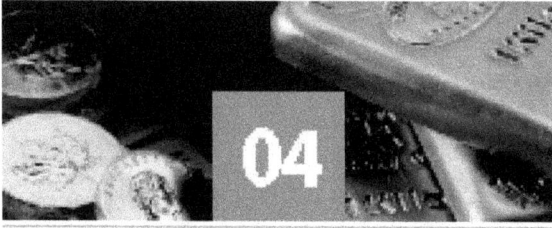

Chapter Four

POWER OF FAITH-FILLED WORDS

"For verily I say unto you, That whosoever shall say unto this mountain, Be thou removed, and be thou cast into the sea; and shall not doubt in his heart, but shall believe that those things which he saith shall come to pass; he shall have whatsoever he saith." (Mark 11:23)

Your faith-filled words have the capacity to procure whatever you want in life! Your creative words can create your desired world. God, the Creator of the universe actually created everything we see today with His words. He spoke creation into existence, and the substance of His faith manifested into what we can now see.

The Word of God spoken in faith has unlimited power. Everything we see was created by words, and it is the very Word of God that holds the universe together. The Bible says, "Who being the brightness of his glory, and the express image of his person, and upholding all things by the word of his power, when he had by himself purged our sins, sat down on the right hand of the Majesty on high;" (Heb. 1:3).

Therefore, everything we see will respond to faith-filled words. If we want to start seeing the power of God manifest in our lives, we will have to start paying attention to what we say. Words have power—more than any of us realize, but we often speak them as though they are meaningless.

Jesus Christ certainly understood the power of words, and He used them to change the natural things around Him. For instance, He used His words to curse the fig tree and it dried up in no distant future! The Bible says, "And seeing a fig tree afar off having leaves, he came, if haply he might find any thing thereon: and when he came to it, he found nothing but leaves; for the time of figs was not yet. And Jesus answered and said unto it, No man eat fruit of thee hereafter for ever. And his disciples heard it."

(Mark 11: 13-14)

"And in the morning, as they passed by, they saw the fig tree dried up from the roots. And Peter calling to remembrance saith unto him, Master, behold, the fig tree which thou cursedst is withered away. And Jesus answering saith unto them, Have faith in God. For verily I say unto you, That whosoever shall say unto this mountain, Be thou removed, and be thou cast into the sea; and shall not doubt in his heart, but shall believe that those things which he saith shall come to pass; he shall have whatsoever he saith. Therefore I say unto you, What things soever ye desire, when ye pray, believe that ye receive them, and ye shall have them."

(Mark 11: 20-24)

Jesus went on to elucidate that this wasn't limited to a fig tree. He used a mountain as an example, but I believe it could apply to anything. He was making the point that if we say it with our mouths and believe it in our hearts, we can have what we say.

He also made it very clear who is qualified to use words in this way: He said, "whosoever shall say." Are you a "whosoever"? I believe you are, then you're qualified, and your words can affect the natural as well as the spiritual world. The words that have power are words that are filled with faith. And it's important to understand that the faith they're filled with is not your human faith.

Luke 6:45 says that what you speak comes from the abundance of your heart. In other words, you speak words that are stored in your heart. The question then is what kind of words do you store in your heart? Faith filled words or fear filled words? Negative words or positive words?

And if you understand that your words have power, then you must watch over your tongue and ensure that you only utter what you want. Are you in need of healing? Just declare, "I believe that I'm healed"

Are you in need of prosperity? Just declare like David, "O Lord, send now prosperity"

"Save now, I beseech thee, O LORD: O LORD, I beseech thee, send now prosperity." (Ps. 118:25)

Are you in need of a job, a child, a breakthrough? Use your mouth to speak out what you want in faith!

It is germane to note that our mouths play a major role in our quest to commanding blessings via our faith. We express our faith via our mouth. We believe in our heart but we express what we believe via our mouth. The Bible says, "But what saith it? The word is nigh thee, even in thy mouth, and in thy heart: that is, the word of faith, which we preach; That if thou shalt confess with thy mouth the Lord Jesus, and shalt believe in thine heart that God hath raised him from the dead, thou shalt be saved. For with the heart man believeth unto righteousness; and with the mouth confession is made unto salvation" (Rom 10:8-10).

If you can't declare your healing, you might die of sickness. The sick must confess he is well. And then he will secure his healing. So many times I feel funny in my body, but my confessions of health and healing have secured my total wellbeing. Confess health! God has given you "a mouth and wisdom which all your adversaries shall not be able to gainsay nor resist" (Luke 21:15).

Declare what you have seen from God's Word confidently and boldly. It is what you declare from the Word that determines your outcome. As God's servant, I have been privileged to have my words or declarations confirmed by God on so many occasions. Just recently, a pregnant woman in our church was finding it difficult to deliver her baby due to closed pelvis. She called me for prayers and I thundered in faith, "Oh you pelvis be opened now in Jesus name." And that was it, the pelvis opened and she delivered safely.

So many Christians are not speaking because of doubt and unbelief. Some are wondering, "What if I say and it does not happen?" Well, say it anyway. Tell yourself: "What if I say it and it happens!" Go ahead and keep saying it until you see the practical manifestation of what you want. In the light of Isaiah 44:26, "That confirmeth the word of his servant, and performeth the counsel of his messengers ..." your onus is to say it, and God's onus is to confirm it. One critical truth is that God does not confirm His servant, He confirms the word of His servant! He does not confirm the qualification of His servant, He confirms the pronouncements of His servant. What God confirms is your word, so give Him enough words to confirm. How I wish every single lady out there will declare only positive words about what she wants to see and not what she sees currently. Let her talk about her marriage not her single-hood. How I wish every student out there will speak success instead of failure. Why must a student use his mouth to say "this subject is so difficult" or "I know I will not pass this course" You shall have whatsoever you say with your mouth!

Many people are not simply consistent in their speaking at all! Today they are speaking positively the next moment they are speaking negatively.

If you spoke faith filled words yesterday, and today you are speaking fear filled words, you have neutralised all the faith you spoke before. Don't be weary in speaking right or positive! The Bible says, "And let us not be weary in well doing: for in due season we shall reap, if we faint not." (Gal 6:9)

Most of the words being communicated today are negative words—words that do not bring about abundant life but cause more problems. The sad truth is that many people have been in the habit of saying negative things that injure their destinies. Some people are even procuring death with their words instead of life. The Bible says, "Death and life are in the power of the tongue: and they that love it shall eat the fruit thereof." (Prov. 18:21)

The Bible says, "Let the weak say, I am strong."

(Joel 3:10) Why will the weak say I am strong when he is weak? The reason is basically because the Bible says, "... He shall have whatsoever he saith" (Mark

11:23). As the weak is saying "I am strong" he would actually become strong.

Bishop David Abioye said, in his book, The Lifestyle of Faith, that "Speaking what you believe means announcing it and announcing it means calling it forth. If for instance you have three children named Abraham, Isaac and Jacob, you don't call Isaac and expect Abraham to answer. When you call Isaac, Isaac answers. Similarly, in the things of the spirit, it is what you call that manifests. God called light and He saw light. Every other thing He called He saw."

The children of Israel were announcing death instead of life. They said that they would have preferred to die in Egypt than to die in the wilderness. And God heard what they said or their confessions; and He promised to do according to their words. "Say unto them, As truly as I live, saith the LORD, as ye have spoken in mine ears, so will I do to you:" (Num 14:28)

God is obligated to do what we say to His hearing!

Your words, like the word of God will not return to you void. Your faith filled words will accomplish results beyond your wildest imagination. "So shall my word be that goeth forth out of my mouth: it shall not return unto me void, but it shall accomplish that which I please, and it shall prosper in the thing whereto I sent it." (Is 55:11)

As God's servant, I am very sensitive and cautious about what I say, for I know that my words are powerful to deliver results, positively or negatively. As such, I cannot afford to be careless about what I say or go about town speaking negatively or cursing people who offend me. Instead I generously say words of blessing to people. It's better that God confirms the blessings I release upon people.

May I conclude this chapter by invoking the Abrahamic blessings upon you, my reader! I declare and decree that you will be richly and greatly blessed in the order of father Abraham in Jesus name! God Almighty will empower you to command and create great wealth like Abraham! His blessings will be much upon you that other people would be testifying on your behalf like the servant of Abraham testified of God's blessings upon his master! "And the LORD hath blessed my master greatly; and he is become great: and he hath given him flocks, and herds, and silver, and gold, and menservants, and maidservants, and camels, and asses."

(Genesis 24:35)

Chapter Five

FAITH FOR CHANGE OF STATUS

"And when Jesus departed thence, two blind men
followed him, crying, and saying, Thou Son of David,
have mercy on us. And when he was come into the
house, the blind men came to him: and Jesus saith
unto them, Believe ye that I am able to do this? They
said unto him, Yea, Lord. Then touched he their
eyes, saying, According to your faith be it unto you."

(Matt 9:27-29)

Change of status is possible. If you are fed up with your current location or station of life, you have the power to change it. If it's your desire to move up the ladder of life, you can. You can get whatever you want out of life through the instrumentality of faith. "Jesus said unto him, If thou canst believe, all things are possible to him that believeth." (Mark 9:23)

When you and I come on the frequency of faith, we operate in the class of God! When you operate faith you cease to exist on the human level. Your status changes to divinity level. "And Jesus looking upon them saith, With men it is impossible, but not with God: for with God all things are possible." (Mark 10:27)

Two blind men experienced a change of story or status when they engaged the force of faith. They wanted to get their sight, and they got it. They were healed according to their faith. Jesus asked them this question: "Believe ye that I am able to do this?" He heard their cry, but He still asked them. He wanted to see their faith at work.

Faith for change of status is about trusting the ability of God to effect the change you desperately want in your life. God, the unchangeable Changer has the ability to change your status. He is the One who changed us "from Darkness" to "Marvellous light."

From "Not a people" to "a people of God" And from people that have "Not obtained mercy" to people who "now have obtained mercy." The Bible says, "But ye are a chosen generation, a royal priesthood, an holy nation, a peculiar people; that ye should shew forth the praises of him who hath called you out of darkness into his marvellous light: Which in time past were not a people, but are now the people of God: which had not obtained mercy, but now have obtained mercy."

(1 Peter 2:9-10)

The one who changed you from a sinner to a saint can change your story or situation today.

Faith for change of status must be anchored on God's faithfulness. The fact that God does not lie should promote our faith in Him. The Bible says, "God is not a man, that he should lie; neither the son of man, that he should repent: hath he said, and shall he not do it? or hath he spoken, and shall he not make it good?" (Num 23:19)

The One who has power to change times and seasons will He not change your status? "And he changeth the times and the seasons: he removeth kings, and setteth up kings: he giveth wisdom unto the wise, and knowledge to them that know understanding:" (Dan 2:21)

Will God who changed Saul to another man in a jiffy, after he met with God's servant, Prophet Samuel, not change your own life? The Bible says, "And the Spirit of the LORD will come upon thee, and thou shalt prophesy with them, and shalt be turned into another man. And let it be, when these signs are come unto thee, that thou do as occasion serve thee; for God is with thee. And thou shalt go down before me to Gilgal; and, behold, I will come down unto thee, to offer burnt offerings, and to sacrifice sacrifices of peace offerings: seven days shalt thou tarry, till I come to thee, and shew thee what thou shalt do. And it was so, that when he had turned his back to go from Samuel, God gave him another heart: and all those signs came to pass that day. And when they came thither to the hill, behold, a company of prophets met him; and the Spirit of God came upon him, and he prophesied among them." (1Sam 10:6-10)

Our Lord Jesus Christ changed water to wine!

He has the power to change your life for the better.

Very soon your mouth will be filled with laughter!

"WHEN the LORD turned again the captivity of Zion, we were like them that dream. Then was our mouth filled with laughter, and our tongue with singing: then said they among the heathen, The LORD hath done great things for them. The LORD hath done great things for us; whereof we are glad. Turn again our captivity, O LORD, as the streams in the south." (Ps 126:1-4)

Faith for change of status must be anchored on what God has done before! "David said moreover, The LORD that delivered me out of the paw of the lion, and out of the paw of the bear, he will deliver me out of the hand of this Philistine. And Saul said unto David, Go, and the LORD be with thee." (1Sam 17:37)

As a believer, do you have a testimony of what God has done before in your life? Has God moved you from one class to another, from one good job to a better job, from one level of influence to another? Has He changed your clothes? I know you are not wearing the same clothes you wore five years ago! God ensured your change of wardrobes. After all the Bible says, "... A man can receive nothing, except it be given him from heaven." (John 3:27)

Whatever you have today God gave them to you, and He is well able to give more to you if you engage your faith.

As believers, we are all waiting for what I will call the "Ultimate change!" I mean the great change from mortality to immortality. A great change from terrestrial to celestial! "Behold, I shew you a mystery; We shall not all sleep, but we shall all be changed, In a moment, in the twinkling of an eye, at the last trump: for the trumpet shall sound, and the dead shall be raised incorruptible, and we shall be changed."

(1 Cor 15:51-52)

Are you really hoping for this great change?

God has promised us this great change and we cannot afford to doubt or disbelieve Him. "The LORD is my portion, saith my soul; therefore will I hope in him. The LORD is good unto them that wait for him, to the soul that seeketh him. It is good that a man should both hope and quietly wait for the salvation of the LORD."

(Lam 3:24-26)

Do you have hope of making heaven or eternal life with God in heaven? "In hope of eternal life, which God, that cannot lie, promised before the world began;" (Titus 1:2)

God cannot lie! He is faithful to His promises! He is dependable! I therefore urge you to place your hope and faith on His finished work on the cross of Calvary for your eternal redemption, this is because your works or self-righteousness will never matter before God on the last day!

Chapter Six

UNDERSTANDING THE PRAYER OF FAITH

"Therefore I say unto you, What things soever ye desire, when ye pray, believe that ye receive them, and ye shall have them." Mark 11:24

Most of us are not aware that there are several types of prayer discussed in God's Word, and if we use one type when we should be using another, our prayers will not be effective or result oriented.

In Matthew 18:19, Jesus introduced the prayer of agreement when He said, "'Again I say to you that if two of you agree on earth concerning anything that they ask, it will be done for them by My Father in heaven'" (NKJV).

To use the prayer of agreement, you must be sure that the person with whom you are agreeing is in line with what you are asking for. If a Christian brother or sister should ask me to agree with him or her in prayers I should be able to ask, "What specifically do you want me to agree or pray about with you? I must make sure I am in perfect agreement with my prayer partner. I must have full knowledge about what we are praying about. When my wife and I got married, I suggested to her the need for us to wait for at least one or two years before having children. I asked that we pray a prayer of agreement to present our request to God, which she did, but was not in full agreement. When we waited more than expected, she started blaming me but later started utilizing the Word of God as tablets given in the hospital. That is, her Word intake on scriptures relating to conception and the promises of God to give her children, became her 'medication', confession, three times daily. This she did concertedly until the physical manifestation of our first son.

There is also prayer of intercession! Intercession means you are interceding—acting in prayer—on behalf of someone else. The person may be incapable of praying for himself or herself. Perhaps he or she is so sick in the hospital and can't muster the energy to pray. Intercession involves praying for others. It may involve praying for your family, church, community and nation. You can stand in the gap for your national leaders in government.

There is another of type of prayer called Prayer of Binding and Loosing as found in

Matthew 18:18-20 "Verily I say unto you, Whatsoever ye shall bind on earth shall be bound in heaven: and whatsoever ye shall loose on earth shall be loosed in heaven. Again I say unto you, That if two of you shall agree on earth as touching any thing that they shall ask, it shall be done for them of my Father which is in heaven. For where two or three are gathered together in my name, there am I in the midst of them."

Please note that Jesus meant that we have authority here on this earth by virtue of our covenant rights and privileges as children of God.

That we are cardinal deciders or initiators, we move heaven to respond to us. That things do not begin in heaven and come to Earth, but rather the action starts here on Earth. Notice that it says, "Whatever you bind on earth will be bound in heaven, and whatever you loose on earth will be loosed in heaven."

We have been empowered to decide what happens on earth. We are ambassadors of heaven and have the authority of our home government to speak and do things with full support and approval of our head of government, God Almighty! We have power to bind foul spirits that are at work in people's lives or loose angelic spirits to work on our behalf in those areas where God has already promised us results. When we pray in this manner, God affirms it in heaven and puts His seal of approval on our prayer. Binding and loosing have to be based on the authority God has granted us in Scripture.

God has provided each type of prayer for a specific purpose. In this chapter I'm going to dwell majorly on the prayer of faith.

What is prayer of faith?

Prayer of faith is a petition prayer. Petition prayer is between you and God. It is you asking Him for a specific, particular thing or outcome. It is you presenting your desires before Him in prayers. It is a formal and personal request that you present before God for His attention and answers. We have some veritable examples of prayer of faith in the Bible. Now let's consider the prayer of Hannah in 1 Samuel 1:11-12 "And she vowed a vow, and said, O LORD of hosts, if thou wilt indeed look on the affliction of thine handmaid, and remember me, and not forget thine handmaid, but wilt give unto thine handmaid a man child, then I will give him unto the LORD all the days of his life, and there shall no razor come upon his head. And it came to pass, as she continued praying before the LORD, that Eli marked her mouth."

"And she said, Oh my lord, as thy soul liveth, my lord, I am the woman that stood by thee here, praying unto the LORD. For this child I prayed; and the LORD hath given me my petition which I asked of him:" (1Samue l 1:26-27)

The Bible says, "Therefore I say unto you, What things soever ye desire, when ye pray, believe that ye receive them, and ye shall have them." (Mark 11:24)

The rule to consider here is when you pray—not after you pray, not when you feel something, not when you see something. When you pray (the moment that you pray) you must believe that you receive what you asked for. Hannah's petition buttresses the fact that we can believe when we pray. She believed God has heard her prayers. This is because after God's servant told her, "Go in peace: and the God of Israel grant thee thy petition that thou hast asked of him." she went her way and did eat some food and was no longer downcast. She entered into her rest! She had a rest of mind as far as the issue of her request was concerned. The Bible says, "For he that is entered into his rest, he also hath ceased from his own works, as God did from his. Let us labour therefore to enter into that rest, lest any man fall after the same example of unbelief." (Heb 4:10-11)

Someone said, "God lives in one eternal now. There is no past or present for Him. But we are temporal beings who live in the context of time." Hannah prayed in faith, by believing that God has immediately given her what she prayed for—in the spirit realm of course. Her Samuel was not physically or materially manifest! It was her faith that drew her Samuel into practical reality. God who answered Hannah is still in the business of answering prayers today, and He will answer your own specific prayer request in line with His Word, but it is your faith that brings that answer out of the spiritual world into the physical world.

How many times in Scripture does Jesus say to someone, "According to your faith"? He referred to people's faith constantly, and even though it was His power that healed them, He always credited their faith with being the catalyst. In fact, when Jesus went to His hometown, we are told that "He did not do many mighty works there because of their unbelief" (Matt. 13:58). Did Jesus suddenly lose His power on that visit to Nazareth? No! His power never changed. What changed? It was the people's level of faith mixed with His power. There is a simple spiritual explanation for this. God will not do something against your will. God cannot violate your free will.

Prayer of faith is a prayer that you pray believing that you have received what you have asked of the Lord, even though you are yet to see the manifestation. Jesus said, "When you pray, believe that you receive them, and you will have them." The only things that you are going to have are the things that you believed that you received when you prayed. Hannah asked God for a "man child" and she got her Samuel. If she did not believe she received her "man child" when she prayed, she would not have gotten her Samuel! God was moved by her faith!

How do we know when we have prayed a prayer of faith?

Frederick K. C. Price, in his book, "How Faith Works" said, "If you prayed and believed that you have received them, you can never pray the second time for them. Because if you pray the second time, you are saying by your praying the second time, that you did not believe that you received them the first time, and that cancels out the prayer."

Every time we pray for the same things again and again, we are simply demonstrating unbelief and we have kind of cancelled our previous prayer. Our prayer of unbelief takes us back to square one. We have to start afresh. If we had believed we received it, then the deed is done, it is sealed, the transaction is over! All we are required to do is to keep thanking and glorifying God until we see what we asked for practically.

Many of us who pray or ask God for certain things over and over are simply praying in unbelief. Period! Traditionally, many of us are used to begging and we think God responds to begging. We have been made to believe that if we beg long enough, He will finally get tired of our asking and give it to us. God only responds to us only on the platform of His will, mercy and our faith! The Bible says, "And this is the confidence that we have in him, that, if we ask any thing according to his will, he heareth us: And if we know that he hear us, whatsoever we ask, we know that we have the petitions that we desired of him." (1John 5:14-15)

Why do we need this type of prayer?

We need to pray this type of prayer because it holds
the key to unlocking all doors. It could be the solution
to any and every challenge or problem that we may
face in life. It could be a major key to getting our
desires met. "Therefore I say unto you, What things
soever ye desire, when ye pray, believe that ye receive
them, and ye shall have them." (Mark 11:24) Who is
speaking in this passage? Jesus Christ Himself, the
anointed Son of the living God! Going by this
passage, we are made to understand that our desires
are important to God, and that we can present our
desires to God in prayers. Jesus is not talking about
God's desires here but our own desires. God wants
you and I to have our own desires.

The Bible says, "Seek ye out of the book of the
LORD, and read: no one of these shall fail, none shall
want her mate: for my mouth it hath commanded,
and his spirit it hath gathered them." (Isaiah 34:16)

There is a scriptural mate of Mark 11:24, in Ps 37:4,
"Delight thyself also in the LORD; and he shall give
thee the desires of thine heart." In this passage, David
talks about the desire of our heart! He is not talking

about God's desire for us as it were, but our own desires for ourselves. But notice the caveat or condition before God responds favourably to our desires: "Delight thyself also in the LORD..." Delight comes before the desire.

This is where so many of us have missed it! We are desperately promoting our desires to the detriment of projecting our delight in God. We are commanded to seek God and His kingdom first, before all things could be added to us. "But seek ye first the kingdom of God, and his righteousness; and all these things shall be added unto you." (Matthew 6:33)

What does it mean to delight yourself in the Lord?

How can you delight in someone you cannot see? The Lord is not a physical Being that you can see like you see a friend. How then can you delight in Him? It means you should delight yourself in His Word. God is present in His Word! God and His Word are one!

The requirement for getting what we want from God is if we care to abide in Christ. In John 15:7, Jesus says, "If ye abide in me, and my words abide in you, ye shall ask what ye will, and it shall be done unto you." The word "abide" in the Greek, literally means, "to live in, settle down in, and take up residence in." If we care to cogitate a while on this we will discover why our desires have not been met by the Lord. We put the cart before the horse! We must dwell in or settle down in God first before placing our desires or demands. First things first! The Bible says, "Those that be planted in the house of the LORD shall flourish in the courts of our God. They shall still bring forth fruit in old age; they shall be fat and flourishing;" (Psalms 92:13-14)

Are you planted or entrenched in the courts of God? Then you are going to flourish! No doubt about it. If you are planted, you are going to delight in or dwell in God. I urge you to be addicted to God's Word. Have a habit of the Word of God. Why do you have to be conversant with the Word? His Word is His will. His Word is your constitution! In it you get to know your rights and privileges, and claim whatever belongs to you, which you have found in the Word.

Are you willing and prepared to live in, abide in, and settle down in His Word? Would you allow His Word to abide in, live in, settle down in and take up residence in you? If yes, then be rest assured that your desires or whatever you want from God in prayers of faith will be delivered to you. Jabez came before God to ask for personal blessings and he was not disappointed. "And Jabez called on the God of Israel, saying, Oh that thou wouldest bless me indeed, and enlarge my coast, and that thine hand might be with me, and that thou wouldest keep me from evil, that it may not grieve me! And God granted him that which he requested." (1 Chronicles 4:10)

God who answered Jabez will also answer you in Jesus name!

07

◆ ◆

Chapter Seven

TAPPING INTO OTHER PEOPLE'S FAITH

"That ye be not slothful, but followers of them who
through faith and patience inherit the promises."
(Hebrews 6:12)

There are people who have attained what we want to
attain and there is no doubt about this, except we
want to deceive ourselves or engage in arrogance.
There are people whose faith has energized them to
command outstanding results in life. If we take a look
around us right now we will see one or two

individuals that have inherited the promises we are longing to inherit. We are enjoined to follow them and imitate their faith and patience. We are to look up to them in our faith journey. Abraham remains our indefatigable father of faith. He is our pattern of faith in the Bible.

No wonder we are enjoined to look unto Abraham."Look unto Abraham your father, and unto Sarah that bare you: for I called him alone, and blessed him, and increased him." (Is. 51:2)

What was the stronghold of Abraham's faith? Obedience is it! It was not just obedience, but delightsome and prompt obedience. When God asked him to get out of his country, his kindred and father's house, he promptly obeyed, even though he never had a clear bearing of his destination.

"NOW the LORD had said unto Abram, Get thee out of thy country, and from thy kindred, and from thy father's house, unto a land that I will shew thee: And I will make of thee a great nation, and I will bless thee, and make thy name great; and thou shalt be a blessing: And I will bless them that bless thee, and curse him that curseth thee: and in thee shall all families of the earth be blessed. So Abram departed, as the LORD had spoken unto him; and Lot went with him: and Abram was seventy and five years old when he departed out of Haran. (Gen. 12:1-4)

Also when he was asked to circumcise every male in his house; Abraham obeyed instantly, that same day! "And Abraham took Ishmael his son, and all that were born in his house, and all that were bought with his money, every male among the men of Abraham's house; and circumcised the flesh of their foreskin in the selfsame day, as God had said unto him."

(Gen. 17:23)

Abraham displayed higher level of obedience when he was asked to sacrifice Isaac, and he promptly obeyed by bundling Isaac for sacrifice. The Bible says, "And the angel of the LORD called unto Abraham out of heaven the second time, And said, By myself have I sworn, saith the LORD, for because thou hast done this thing, and hast not withheld thy son, thine only son: That in blessing I will bless thee, and in multiplying I will multiply thy seed as the stars of the heaven, and as the sand which is upon the sea shore; and thy seed shall possess the gate of his enemies; And in thy seed shall all the nations of the earth be blessed; because thou hast obeyed my voice." (Gen.22:15-18)

Abraham left for us a pattern of obedience. His rare obedience committed God to bless him. My beloved reader, your obedience will always commit God and will also provoke His enduring and generational blessings. There is no substitute for obedience in the school of faith.

You and I can tap into other people's testimonies of faith and get what we want from God. There are heroes of faith who have walked or are walking with God with proofs. Such individuals can become our veritable patterns or templates that we can learn from and tap into their faith. I have tapped into my mentor and father in the Lord, Bishop David Oyedepo's faith on so many occasions. His faith steps have motivated me to take certain steps in faith with remarkable proofs.

Are there faith driven people around you? You need faith mentors, I mean men and women of faith that can impart you with the spirit of faith, so that you too may achieve what they are achieving. God is no respecter of persons, what He's done for one person, He can do for another person too.

I was blessed by the story shared by daddy GO, the General Overseer of Redeemed Christian Church of God, Pastor E A Adeboye how he too tapped into the faith-work of others and commanded similar or even greater results in his ministry.

Below is an excerpt of his story:

"I have told you before that when in 1979 when I attended Kenneth Hagin Camp Meeting and I saw about 17,000 people in one place I said, "Oh God! You must do this for me in Nigeria! 17000 people must gather in my Convention!" That time if I had only 17 hundred I will be happy. Then 2 or 3 years later I went to Korea and saw Yongi Cho's church. I saw about almost 500,000 people gathering together in one place. I told God I don't want 17,000 anymore, if You can do this for Yongii Cho You can do it for me! We thank God He's already done that one! And then I kept on expanding my vision. I began to tell my Pastors – in every town within five minutes distance there must be a church, a Redeemed Christian Church of God! They thought it is impossible but I've already seen it! Now, if you drive through Awolowo Road – count the number of churches there! I just mentioned just one street! But I've already expanded my vision beyond that one - the day I heard that Coca-Cola said that very soon in every home there will be somebody who drinks Coca-Cola in the whole world. I changed my vision and have said, in every home, in the whole world, there must be a member of

Redeemed Christian Church of God. I have seen it! And God said if I can see it I can have it!"

Beloved reader, I don't know what you are believing God for right now, and I don't know the level of your faith. But what I know is that God is powerful and faithful to do for you what He has done or doing for others. These individuals are carriers of the spirit of faith which you can tap into for your good. Bishop David Oyedepo went to Oral Roberts University, Tulsa Oklahoma, USA and tapped into the grace and spirit of faith that established the university. Today, Covenant University which God enabled Bishop to establish is a validation of transference of the spirit of grace and faith, as CU is patterned after ORU!

The Bible says, "We having the same spirit of faith, according as it is written, I believed, and therefore have I spoken; we also believe, and therefore speak;" (2Cor. 4:13)

The same spirit of faith in which our faith mentors operated in, can bring us also under the same heavenly influence, that can trigger us to declare what we believe affirmatively and authoritatively. For instance, Caleb operated the spirit of faith which helped him to follow God fully. "But my servant

Caleb, because he had another spirit with him, and hath followed me fully, him will I bring into the land whereinto he went; and his seed shall possess it."

(Number 14:24)

Contemporarily, it was the spirit of faith, not word of faith that provoked Bishop David Oyedepo to declare that the Faith Tabernacle, (the largest church auditorium in the world) was going to be built within one year. And it came to pass!

My sincere prayer is that God Almighty may impart you with the spirit of faith to keep you moving gracefully and tenaciously with His agenda, plan and purpose for your life. May the spirit of faith keep you going strong, so that even when others are giving up, you will be soaring like the eagles!

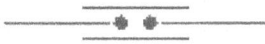

Chapter Eight

PREVENTING FAITH FAILURE

"And the Lord said, Simon, Simon, behold, Satan hath desired to have you, that he may sift you as wheat: But I have prayed for thee, that thy faith fail not: and when thou art converted, strengthen thy brethren." (Luke 22:31-32)

In the passage above, Jesus gave us a hint that faith has the propensity to fail. The sad truth is that many Christians have suffered faith failure. Many have left their robust spiritual heritage and are now running after the things of the world! What a shame! Understanding that your faith could fail would provoke you to take measures to prevent faith failure. To stop Peter's faith from failing, the Master prayed for him, "... I have prayed for thee that thy faith faileth not ..." In the entire Bible, Jesus prayed for just an individual and that person was Peter. Jesus' prayer goes to show the importance of putting measures in place against faith failure.

Faith failure is dangerous to your destiny and general wellbeing. If your faith fails, even God may find it difficult to help you. Why? Because He needs your faith currency to give you what you want. In this book I have repeatedly asserted that with faith in proper position or proper alignment, you can get what you want from God. Now, how will you get things from God if your faith fails to work. It's like heart failure. If a person's heart fails, that's a very precarious condition you know, the person may not function normally and he may even die.

John the Baptist was in faith when he declared: "I saw the Spirit descending from heaven like a dove, and it abode upon him. And I knew him not: but he that sent me to baptize with water, the same said unto me, Upon whom thou shalt see the Spirit descending, and remaining on him, the same is he which baptizeth with the Holy Ghost. And I saw, and bare record that this is the Son of God. Again the next day after John stood, and two of his disciples; And looking upon Jesus as he walked, he saith, Behold the Lamb of God!" (John 1:32-36)

But the same John the Baptist started questioning and doubting the true identity of Jesus Christ. "Now when John had heard in the prison the works of Christ, he sent two of his disciples, And said unto him, Art thou he that should come, or do we look for another?"

(Mat 11:2-3)

I presume that John the Baptist suffered faith failure, maybe because of the excruciating pain he was going through in the prison. It is even possible that he was expecting Jesus to intervene in his trouble with King Herod. He became offended in the very Person he publicly affirmed. Jesus' reply validates the popular opinion that John was offended in Him. The Bible says, "Jesus answered and said unto them, Go and shew John again those things which ye do hear and see: The blind receive their sight, and the lame walk, the lepers are cleansed, and the deaf hear, the dead are raised up, and the poor have the gospel preached to them. And blessed is he, whosoever shall not be offended in me."

(Mat 11:4-6)

May we not find ourselves in a situation where we will doubt or question our Lord and Savior! Amen!

According to Bishop David Abioye, "Faith is our spiritual arrowhead. If the head of an arrow is off what can the body do? Virtually nothing! In every spiritual battle, faith is the first attacker that tells the devil to clear off." Are we surprised that the enemy is after our faith? Faith is the major weapon which we engage to fight the enemy. In Ephesians 6:16, Apostle Paul says, "Above all, taking the shield of faith..." Faith is superior to other arsenals of spiritual weapons. It is above others! The major reason satan desires to have you is so that he can get rid of your faith and go ahead to destroy your destiny. Like he did to John the Baptist! Imagine for a moment if John had maintained his faith in Christ by inviting Him to speak a word of deliverance. The story would have been different.

My beloved reader, as long as your faith is in place, the devil can never displace you. Until your faith fails, nothing fails! You are not a loser until your faith is lost, hence the need to contend for your faith. The Bible says, "Beloved, when I gave all diligence to write unto you of the common salvation, it was needful for me to write unto you, and exhort you that ye should earnestly contend for the faith which was once delivered unto the saints." (Jude 1:3)

We have been called upon to "earnestly contend for the faith which was once delivered unto the saints." The question is why do we need to contend for our faith? The answer is simple: Christianity loses its relevance without faith. Outside of faith there is no Christianity! We must contend for our faith to prevent any faith failure or wreckage.

Faith is a powerful weapon we use to engage the enemy in a fight. No wonder, he hunts for our faith weapon! He wants to disarm and dispossess us of it and render us vulnerable. Satan dispossessed John the Baptist of his faith and wrecked his destiny! He will not succeed in your own life in Jesus name!

Satan knows very well that our faith is our most cherished and powerful weapon, hence his furious and ferocious attacks on our faith. We must not allow him! We must not surrender our weapon of faith! We must hold firm to our faith and fight the good fight of faith. Whatever we believe God for, we must insist on it, and never to shift ground until it is delivered to us. A couple of years ago, we were believing God for some increase but due to circumstances beyond our control we could not insist on our faith. Just like Peter we lost focus or we shifted our eye of faith from the Lord and His faithful word, and our faith could not deliver results. Remember that Peter lost focus while walking on water, and he began to sink. Satan's greatest strategy is to have our faith sink into the water of nothingness and uselessness. We must resist him ferociously!

But why does satan attack our faith so ferociously?

Satan knows that we can please God significantly via our faith. Heb 11:6 says, "... For without faith it is impossible to please God." And he does not want us to please God! He is happy to see us perennially displeasing God through unbelief and a lifestyle of sin. Don't forget it's the devil's sole ministry to cause us to displease God! And if we are unable to please God, how can we provoke or command His blessings.

The enemy is after our faith because he does not want us to subdue him and his kingdom. "Who through faith subdued kingdoms, wrought righteousness, obtained promises, stopped the mouths of lions," (Hebrews 11:33). The devil is very much aware that by our faith we can cheaply bring him and his demons under our control. With faith, all his fiery darts can be quenched or neutralized.

The devil also knows that by our faith we can take delivery of our inheritance in Christ, we can possess our possession. We can obtain God's promises like father Abraham. Faith is our purchasing currency in the realms of the spirit, so the enemy wants to stop us from making any transaction.

We can prevent faith failure by engaging in regular and heartfelt prayers. Just as Jesus prayed for Peter's faith not fail, and his faith was salvaged from faith failure, we too can engage the power of prayers to stop faith failure. Our prayer can move God except it is not done in faith. The Bible says, "Jesus answered and said unto them, Verily I say unto you, If ye have faith, and doubt not, ye shall not only do this which is done to the fig tree, but also if ye shall say unto this mountain, Be thou removed, and be thou cast into the sea; it shall be done. And all things, whatsoever ye shall ask in prayer, believing, ye shall receive." (Mat 21:21-22)

As powerful as faith is, it will ever need prayer support for fortification and sustainability. The Bible says, "But ye, beloved, building up yourselves on your most holy faith, praying in the Holy Ghost" (Jude 1:20). As we all know, the Holy Spirit driven or Holy Spirit assisted prayer commands greater and faster results, so let us painstakingly engage His help and support as we pray to stop every faith failure. And may our valuable currency of faith be strong enough to procure all our greatest heart desires in Jesus mighty name!`

OTHER BOOKS BY THE AUTHOR

- Get Motivated! Who says you can't make it?
- Hebrew Women's Style
- Young but Mighty
- Child Neglect: is the Church Guilty
- How to Obtain Favour from God and Man
- Understanding Courtship and Pre-marital issues
- Questions Young People Ask- Vol.1
- Essentials of Career Choice
- Strategies for Stress free Relationships
- Becoming a Celebrated Youth (Youth & Success)
- Can Boys and Girls also go to Hell
- Teenagers and Relationships
- Youth and Friendship
- Youth and Opportunity
- Striving for Excellence
- The Youth God Uses
- Building an Effective Youth Ministry
- Pathways to Blissful Courtship
- Enjoying God's Mercy

www.ingramcontent.com/pod-product-compliance
Lightning Source LLC
Chambersburg PA
CBHW071906020426
42331CB00010B/2687